spot

BACKYARD ANIMALS

SKUNKS

by Wendy Strobel Dieker

AMICUS | AMICUS INK

den

kits

Look for these
words and pictures
as you read.

stripes

tail

It is night.
Who is peeking out?
A skunk.

Look at the den. It is a hole. Skunks sleep there during the day.

den

Look at the kits.
They stay in the den
for eight weeks.

kits

stripes

Look at the skunk's stripes.
Skunks have black and white fur.
Some skunks have spots.

tail

Look at the skunk's tail.
The skunk is scared.
Its tail goes up.

The skunk sprays an oily liquid.

It is stinky!

Enemies stay away.

Now the skunk digs.
It finds bugs.
What a good meal!

Look at the den. It is a hole.
Skunks sleep there during the day.

den

den

Look at the kits.
They stay in the den
for eight weeks.

kits

kits

Did you find?

stripes

'stripes

Look at the skunk's stripes.
Skunks have black and white fur.
Some skunks have spots.

tail

tail

Look at the skunk's tail.
The skunk is scared.
Its tail goes up.

Spot is published by Amicus and Amicus Ink
P.O. Box 1329, Mankato, MN 56002
www.amicuspublishing.us

Library of Congress Cataloging-in-Publication Data
Names: Dieker, Wendy Strobel, author.
Title: Skunks / by Wendy Strobel Dieker.
Description: Mankato, Minnesota : Amicus, [2018] | Series:
   Spot. Backyard animals | Audience: Grade K-3.
Identifiers: LCCN 2016044427 (print) | LCCN 2017000794
   (ebook) | ISBN 9781681510965 (library binding) | ISBN
   9781681511863 (e-book) | ISBN 9781681522210 (pbk.)
Subjects: LCSH: Skunks--Juvenile literature.
Classification: LCC QL737.C248 D54 2018 (print) | LCC
   QL737.C248 (ebook) | DDC 599.76/8--dc23
LC record available at https://lccn.loc.gov/2016044427

Printed in the United States of America

HC   10 9 8 7 6 5 4 3 2 1
PB   10 9 8 7 6 5 4 3 2 1

Rebecca Glaser, editor
Deb Miner, series designer
Ciara Beitlich, book designer
Holly Young, photo researcher

Photos by Dreamstime, 2, 10–11, 15;
Getty Images 2, 8–9, 14, 15; iStock
cover, 1, 2, 6–7, 15, 16; Shutterstock 3,
12–13; SuperStock 2, 4–5, 15

SKUNKS